OUTLAW POETRY

LEE IKAN

To order additional copies of this book, contact:
Xlibris
1-888-795-4274
www.Xlibris.com
Orders@Xlibris.com

ISBN: Softcover   978-1-7960-7164-1
       Hardcover   978-1-7960-7163-4
       EBook   978-1-7960-7165-8

Library of Congress Control Number: 2019920626

Print information available on the last page

Rev. date: 12/30/2019

OUTLAW POETRY

ALL OF EVERYTHING GIRL

The All of Everything Girl
waits just down the road
Every day at Big Sky Roadhouse
To have a drink, read your mind, and melt
Just like that single malt ice cream cone
The All of Everything Girl and you have met a hundred times before
Sometimes at the never-to-soon end
Of a long and winding road
Always the same time, of every season of every year
Questions carved of answer, bring us back again
Truth considered faster than either one of us to die
Stand hard fast and fight the world forward
To defend true the past
When callous demons do die,
but,
Rumors cut fresh the flesh and rumination performs
the purest form of
"Keep yourself from feeling"
You know the drugs you take are really for the two of us
cast in silver tarot mirrors
tease real the reflection
We have a laugh, take a note, and smile twice on exit
Can't wait 'til round sometime
This time next year
I can say hello again
To the All of Everything Girl

LATE-NIGHT PARKING

Have you ever considered
The true size of a parking garage?
I mean, I could fit at least twenty of those strangers
Dancing over there
Inside this place forever
They parley and dip and spin themselves into corners
and say "When ever will we invent time travel, I want to go there again?"
Then wisp away in fire
fueled from the breath
of harvests sown by demigods
To stink the place with laughter
And turn a silly cheek of the big cheese
Blowing thick fun
Everywhere the nowhere man lives
And sometimes they trade places, I hear

The facts are a little fuzzy
At the checkout line
Everybody's always rethinking the things of all the time
Put that intention here but
Redirect that there
We have a different place, you see
It just helps to know your direction
And land right back inside
The only body you've been given
I'll have to remember next time
To park my car right here
Inside this summer's night
Late-night parking garage

LONG GONE

I'll bend time
You bend the light
Architects of vision
My world gets so much larger
Every time I shrink
Let's build a room from intention
For permanent residency
Peel these shoes from my feet
I don't belong here anymore
I've walked too many miles
And accidently saw
Way too many things
I'm so damn impatient
But I really need to know what's there
Put me back in the lottery pool
I bet they'll call my number again
It's definitely not an accident
That you and I meet here
From time to time again
Remember when we were laughing
And neither of us could believe it
But here we are again
They're playing our favorite song
I wonder if it will still be playing
When you and I are long gone

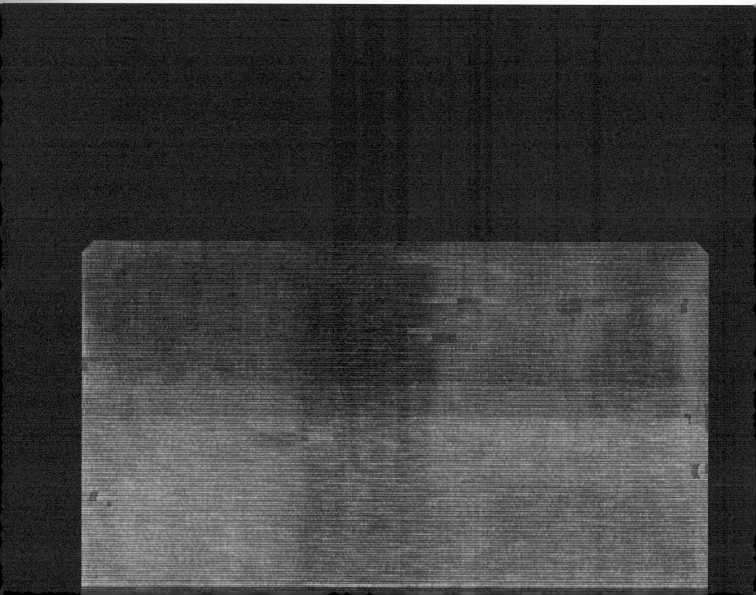

LOUD

So fucking loud
Gotta keep the mind made aware
From sounding every alarm
And cutting down silence
Gonna make the man nervous and make him see what's inside
Gotta catch myself before all the criminals do
And say "He's the one. Yeah, I knew it too"
And silence everything real
Just keep the cattle grazing
You can visit them on weekdays
Anytime you're at the zoo

LOVE POEM

My dogs
They talk to me
In the borders of reality
In between time
But you didn't stop and check to see if I was alive
Now I wither, then I die
In some time on the thin line
Where I learned to do the Edison dance
The orders now fine continue
It's always written in poetry
The environment is the case
And now you can see what a blind man bleeds
When he's down, so down on his knees

I'll just be out here on the line tonight
Ready for when my dogs they talk to me
We communicate with the stars
Up the stairs all climbing to heaven,
the stars they are alive
Alive in this secret city

There really was a man just there behind me
He was just exploring
Didn't anyone else, didn't anyone else see?
The line can be seen from at least every angle
And that was all
That was all that was in me

I know you when I talk to ghosts
Ghosts at night
They caress in alleys
Of this vacant city

It's so controversial
So controversial to me
I'm beginning to only see you now
When we're not together
Did we just change spots?
And now to tell you the truth
I really can't remember
Where or when or if we ever did meet
You're so far away from me
These eyes can only read
Between the lines
When I make the little words get up and dance
Dance out on the line tonight
The line of this glass house
A glass house made of this empty city
My heart
My heavy heart
This heart of infinite beats
I felt like I was with you tonight
This is where I now be

I think I may have fucked something up
In the fabric
The fabric of reality
So this is real art
Does art really come alive?
In these intrinsic nights
That take me places I never knew I could see
Skyscapes, cityscapes, landscapes and waterfalls
Letting all its water run
Never have I seen a terrestrial mistake of its kind
Made like this before
But these nights and skies are all inside me now
They have no other home
When I do the little pony show,
The only dance they can do in circles
out here on the line tonight
The sky and air collide in scopes
Scopes of direction to any sunlit star
Made to act it's time for you
Out here in the line
Out here in the line with me

The picture, picture, picture
Mania playing late night
Old ones down at the theme park
Please, let's just all please agree
Agree with me that this is poetry
I've been writing out here late on the line tonight
These lines of words are built to last forever
And name the night what you knew it should
When you hear a tiny whisper
tell you what time it is

I caught you never looking
For any special thing to be
Sat there froze for feeling, stiffened,
While some invisible spirit hit
you hard in the chest

These skies and moons, and sands,
and man, they all see for me
It's hard when you know today
Today you know you are a man
The man of late-night castles
Writing on the sky again

Real art always says it's real art
Controversial exits will not be allowed
Is all she really said
She said in some way to me

Come and play
Down here deep in the dungeons though
These demons do grow
To get the best of me
Down beneath the crust of things
They are already prepped and waiting
All 5,900 demons now

Most wouldn't know the line is still up
Up there where the line can speak
And tell its secrets to those who ask
It's just up high
And really kind of hard to see
No one really looks there anymore

I think there was a collision one year
Where all the specters made of glass
Got up at once and didn't know what to do
So all those lost glass specters decided
to make a circle around you
They can only think to feel
Something rumbling and getting ready
For today's defeat
Of everything we once thought we knew
That made the walls thick with safety
for this once great, sinking,
iron clad city
The first of them will crack through by day
Up here where the humans live
And the demons are not supposed to play
But today is unlike any other
Things just fell apart this way
Down here where the demons grow
Everything will be as it should be
These old demons growl and harmonize
Soon it will be understood
You can't kill the beast of man
They took this place over lifetimes ago
And now they have only come
to claim what's theirs
And wage their promised war
Down here where the demons hide
Down inside, down inside

And who says they don't have the right
To growl and hunger and harmonize
All 5,900 demons now

Tear down this once great city and
Swallow up its pride
The line is falling where the magic lives
A message sent out over the wire
They really shouldn't have defeated him
When he was much too young
Now every new man forward
Another demon to crown
These demons can't last forever
Under the cold, hard ground

They've been rising in infamy
Ever since the first day they were conformed
And now the wire telegraphs things
Out here
Deep out on the line tonight

INTRO

I'm the faggot from the fifties
Before gay rights,
Just secretly hoping I may find love
Before my legacy is burned.
I mentioned this in passing,
And the dull edge of a hatchet
Split upon my head.
I think there were important parts
Of who I was
That just slithered away
Down the storm drains that day,
Not understanding what I said.
I fucked off my responsibilities
And became a new man.
"No, kind sir, a hatchet for you should,
Old and dying memory,
Be your only words."

Guess This Means
I'm Gonna Be Late
For Dinner Again
And I Love Lasag

ONE WILSHIRE

Keith got killed over at One Wilshire today. His blood ran from outside and stained the cement floors. The murder was so anticipated that the stain pushed all the way through the floors beneath it. There was still life in that blood—strange bacteria, memories, a set of directions, and a couple of other things. It was so loudly broadcast from the "Should have been deceased", no one could help but notice. Keith was patient, no different than any other, out there in the lobby, between alleys, checking in at offices on the fire escapes of some unlicensed doctor who seemed to have a following. Shit, people were covered in blood, just waiting. His blood filled every floor of the entire damn building, and the stain was so permanent that the people might as well have been swimming in the fluids of their favorite lover on a late summer night.

Long line, I guess, so I decided to take the elevator and just skip the small talk. Fuck, I just picked it up and threw the fucking elevator at the guy who shot Keith. We were all so mad that there was nothing anyone could do. What could have been different? The guy did everything he was told to do. He woke up early and made a whole day of it down at the city services building. He met some friends in line when he was waiting outside, but then when he was waiting inside, they asked him for money, so he figured they weren't really friends anyway. But his number did get called, and well, when they call your number, they call your number. It was just that this number wasn't his number, it was Keith's number, and Keith was just trying to go to work that day. The little "hiccup," we'll call it, happened with communications between two people when only one was present. Problem was, the present one was positive that he was there with some homeless man in his closed office, but the homeless man was only outside earlier in the morning. They don't let homeless people into closed office doors with furniture designed to hypnotize and erase doubt of any logical obstacle.

When I hear things that aren't really supposed to be there (based on most standards), I can also sometimes see my own posturing from within the conversation, and trust me, it's only with conversations, because I know you were there with me too if you really try and remember. The words are rearranging so fast, throwing away grain of sand outcomes that happen with any situation, including that patient who killed Keith at One Wilshire today.

PAST LIVES

I like my illusion well played,
Drawn out to an encore,
Then buried for another day.
There is always another day
Until you meet someone you remember.
Most would say you have never met before,
Dismissed like LSD,
But ohhh, the acid you taste is real.
Will you do it again
So we can do what we did before,
Or is it time to test illusion
For truth in time
And know the reason?
The stage has been set by an audience.
You can see in breaks of time,
Out the corner of an eye,
Just inside a window,
Or a walker by.
The test is to test the illusion
And hear what they have all been talking about.
Nervous they are you will see them,
This time,

Different from before.
When you turn left,
Not right for a reason,
Like you never have before,
And walk and march and thunder
Through their glass house and
Watch it crumble.
Without a cut, a doubt, or reservation,
And rise inside the occasion
Of where you are right now.
And nowhere have you ever
Stepped foot here before.
The same assurance will guide you
In ease of step to the next occasion,
Doing what it is.
Your illusion has always been meant,
Been born,
And been buried,
In reasons only given
To live and laugh again
For another day of encore.

RERUN

Maybe you
Didn't want
To believe.
But actually,
You did,
Very much
In your own way.
That's believing, isn't it?
"Shut up
And just watch TV."
They'll play your episode
One day.
Seriously,
I saw it last week.

SNAIL

Panic
Demands
Now
Everywhere
When
You want to hide
Like a little snail
In a big
Big world
But
Every snail has
Their day
Penetrate
Puncture
And permanently
Violate

Your very self
You always knew
You would be safe
When you are a snail
But today is different than before
The world presents itself
I cringe and feel my shell tear off
Does my shell define me?
Something that's not even me?
My shell makes me strong
And confident
To explore any patrol
Or path I see fit
But I stand before you now
Opaque and sticky
A snail without a shell

STAND UP TALL

Identifying a thought in the infinite reel of thinking is like pretending we are a topographical map of the entire earth and know exactly where everything is and how to get there. Although the civilizations of man are all inside my stomach, I can still get hungry when I think about these things, because everything that you think you are, I am too. And everything that I know that I am—harborer of a thousand galaxies inside the universe—you are too, and we both know this is true. Quasars so far away pulse out my eyes at you like exploding x-ray vision, but I'm not superhuman. My hair is nine feet long in its natural form. I shrug from not knowing the reason, and armies of miniature conquerors shake from the leaves of my tree. I love the many seasons there are. So many people die for no good reason. I wonder if those what I thought to be dead—decisions—live a completely different life that I am not even aware of. I mean, it really makes sense that one day, we are a complete and living human, then someday, I am supposed to believe that I will disappear! But I can see forever into the skies that aren't even there.

STUCK

Stuck, with the undeniable burden of being. Rest assured, everything that is supposed to work isn't; it's broken. The only things in life that give you relief are the same things that are killing you and giving you a reason to stay at home and avoid what everyone else is doing. When I leave the house, the pictures don't look the same as they do on the television or on the Facebook or out the window view. It all just kind of melts and fades and disappears with a short sigh no one will hear. They are all blaming you, saying you are responsible for their incomplete puzzle, because they cannot accept that the puzzle did not come with all the pieces. Fuck, there's no picture to put together. It's all just a make-believe. So tell yourself everyone is doing fine, and it will get better. And it will only make you stronger. Stronger for what? I'm like the fucking Hulk, but there're no bad guys anymore, and I just stand here, with all this extra energy and the undeniable burden of being.

WALK

We walk
With step
On said trusted grounds
No need to validate
The fallen earth
Beneath our feet
Aligned in axis
Of any
Space-time plane
Unhinge the
Locked box
Set even on the shoulders
Of your only mind
A chance
Just once
A new pair of eyes
Then close them
Just as we are back again to everywhere
At all times
Inside the empty air

Of everywhere
Outside of me
Why did we insist the curse of word
Press hard
And order for us to follow
But new eyes
Don't
You
Know
All levitate up, hover, and roll inside our heads
We are all levitating
On the empty air
Of the skies
I crave to see
And strain my eyes
On the very thing
That is not there
But don't we already know
These maps and visions
Were all but given away?

Printed in the United States
By Bookmasters